WRITING TIPS WORKBOOK

A CREATIVE AND PRACTICAL GUIDE TO IMPROVING YOUR STORY (THE CREATIVE WRITER'S TOOLKIT BOOK 2)

MERRIE DESTEFANO

RUBY SLIPPERS PRESS

CONTENTS

AUTHOR'S AWARDS

MERRIE DESTEFANO

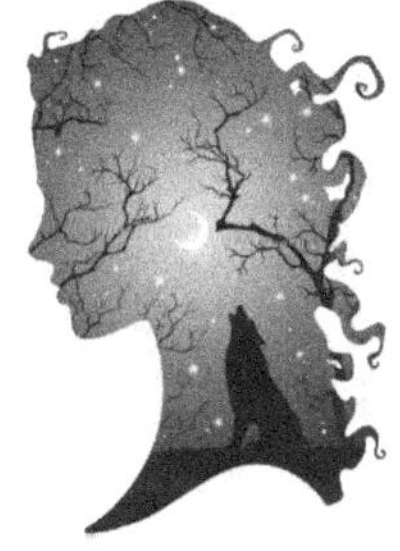

Realm Award Winner
Paranormal/Horror
Shade: The Complete Trilogy
2019 Realm Makers Awards

Silver Medal Winner
YA Horror/Mystery
Shade: The Complete Trilogy
2019 Moonbeam Children's Book Awards

Second Place Winner
YA/NA Speculative Fiction
Valiant
2019 YARWA Athena Awards

Writer Of The Year
Merrie Destefano
2010 Mount Hermon Writer's Conference

WRITING TIPS
"A jewel for all writers of speculative fiction, shining light on hidden facets of the writing process."—Laura Bickle, author of the Wildlands series

"Great for aspiring scribes and writers starting out, but also very useful for experienced writers looking for new ways to brainstorm and deepen their stories."—Paul A. Rose Jr.

"*Writing Tips* is a short and succinct guide that should become the staple of any aspiring writer's arsenal."—Aden

"It's organized clearly and to the point, which I appreciate greatly as a writer who's constantly busy meeting deadlines."—Silvana

"This quick, simple read sparked story ideas, broke my internal logjam, and ultimately got me started on my next book."—Bradley D Huebert

"This book by Merrie Destefano is filled to the brim with tricks, tips, and tools to make writing a book much easier."—Sapphyria

"Merrie shares the key strategies and rules-of-thumb that she uses to craft her stories and make them so appealing to readers." —Teddi Deppner

"Merrie Destefano's *Writing Tips* is filled with gems like "story is king" and "secret world-building tips." She reveals the multi-layered depth of her thinking process which has always held me in awe of her creative talent."—Frequent Shopper

SHADE: The Complete Trilogy

"Uniquely haunting and dangerous—my best read of the year so far!"—Rachel Marks, best-selling author of *Darkness Brutal*

"Haunting imagery, electrical tension—will appeal to fans of Ransom Riggs' *Miss Peregrine's Home For Peculiar Children*."—Aden Polydoros, author of *The City Beautiful*

VALIANT

"An imaginative, fresh take on the time travel novel."—Tosca Lee, NYT-bestselling author of *The Progeny*

"*Edge of Tomorrow* meets *Terminator* in this riveting, post-apocalyptic adventure from Merrie Destefano."—Paul Regnier, author of the *Space Drifter* series

"With its high tension and non-stop action, this book is perfect for fans of THE 5TH WAVE and DIVERGENT."—Aden Polydoros, author of *The City Beautiful*

LOST GIRLS

"A concise, bold crime tale that, even in its darkest moments, shines with brilliance." -*Kirkus Reviews*

"A book that parents, teachers and law-enforcement officers should read, as well as young adults."—Anita Ojeda, Educator at Holbrook Indian School

"I highly suggest you run out the door right now and go buy it. This novel was a delightful YA surprise that I enjoyed from beginning to end."—Sydney West, Sydney's Shelves

INTRODUCTION

I recently put myself on a new schedule, which included tackling old projects as well as new, and as a result, I discovered that I had several books almost finished.

This little book was one of them.

Maybe, like me, you're at a point where you want to take your creative life back and get serious about your work again.

For me, that means I'm also getting serious about helping other writers.

That's been a goal of mine for a very long time.

This workbook is a companion to the digital book of the same name. However, the print version contains more. Besides exercises, tips, and writing prompts, there are also lined pages for you to write upon—making the print version uniquely yours. Also, just so you know, I don't write to market, so you won't find those sorts of tips in any of my upcoming writing books. There are many talented, proven experts out there with wonderful books on that subject. I'm just not one of them.

My focus is on writing the best story possible, while

creating believable characters and well-developed worlds along the way. In this book, I'll be offering some tips, thoughts, and ideas that helped me, and I hope they'll encourage other writers as well, because publishing can be a difficult business.

The best way to write a story?

One word at a time. Until they flow off your page and turn into a book.

Let me just say 'Hurrah to you!' if you're writing! I'm cheering for you!

Blessings always,

Merrie Destefano

CHAPTER ONE: HOW ORGANIC WRITING CAN MAKE YOUR STORY SEEM MORE REAL.

EVERYTHING SEEMS TO BE GOING ORGANIC lately—from produce in the grocery store to fabrics in your clothing to ingredients in your soap. Even books, which seemed pretty organic to me to begin with since they were made from paper, are now available in a more earth-friendly version—electronic.

Personally, as a health nut and a person with multiple allergies, I like this organic revolution and I hope it's here to stay.

. . .

BUT WHAT ABOUT YOUR WRITING?

What if you took this whole organic process a step further and applied it to your writing, specifically as it relates to world-building? To readers of science fiction, fantasy, and horror, world-building is crucial to creating a believable story, right? When we buy a book, we expect the world to have a natural, realistic, believable structure or we don't want to read it. And that's the last thing we, as writers, want—for someone to put down our book because one element didn't ring true.

BELOW IS A LIST OF SECRET, ORGANIC, WORLD-BUILDING RULES THIS WRITER LIVES BY:

1. Set up your world so that it can have a natural evolution.

For instance, try changing just one thing within your existing world—like P. D. James did in *The Children of Men*, where suddenly, no one could have children—then see how, over time, that one change could affect everything else in the world.

EXERCISE 1: What one thing could you change in your current WIP (work in progress) that would not only make a big difference, but would improve the story? You can brainstorm ideas below:

____

____

2. These changes could be subtle or they could be drastic.

Spend time considering how this one change could influence the culture, from politics to religion to social mores. In my book, *Afterlife*, I created a technology where we could resurrect instead of die and this had a trickle-down effect on nearly everything, including major world religions. I didn't realize it until I started working on the book, but death is a very significant part of our lives.

EXERCISE 2: Take that first idea and expand on it a little bit more. How would it affect the politics in your story? Would everyone in your society agree or would some people object to this change? How would this difference of opinion show itself?

____

____

____

____

____

____

____

3. Reveal these changes to the reader.

Do it carefully, gently, clue by clue, throughout your story. Reveal the world in bits and pieces, a little snippet here and there. Make it a mystery and remove the veil, one layer at a time. This way the reader is never overwhelmed or pulled out of the story. Remember, story is king. All the pretty writing and deep, tortured characters in the world cannot replace story.

EXERCISE 3: Think about how you can reveal these changes a little bit at a time. Which changes would your reader notice right away and which ones would need to be revealed later? Would you show these to the reader or reveal them in dialogue? Practice a few different ways to unveil these changes below.

____

____

____

____

____

____

____

____

4. Your characters should not be surprised by this different world.

They won't be amazed by flying cats or talking squirrels. With the exception of a visitor from another time or planet, your characters will have lived in this world for their entire lives. If anything, they will be jaded, weary, frustrated and irritated by it—not surprised. Just like we get irritable when we're stuck in traffic, they might get irritable if they have to wait two weeks for a skin graft that would allow them to grow a third arm.

EXERCISE 4: Give an example below of something unusual that could happen in this world that the inhabitants would take for granted. Make sure you give your characters the proper reaction and emotions. Remember they won't be startled if this is something they've dealt with for years.

____

____

____

____

____

____

5. Your metaphors and similes must be in keeping with your new and different world.

For instance, you can't use a phrase like, "The days flew past, like pages turning in a book," if your story takes place in a culture where everything is written on scrolls. Likewise, if your main character is a dog who lives on Venus, he isn't going to think about Astro on the *Jetsons*.

EXERCISE 5: Give some examples of new phrases and expressions and terminology that could be used in this different world.

____

____

____

____

____

____

____

____

____

6. When built correctly, your world should have a domino effect.

One thing will cause another thing to happen and so on. Keep the big picture in mind at all times. Even though you may be writing a story that feels like a microcosm—because it involves only a few characters and takes place over a few days in time—remember that there's always a macrocosm lurking behind it. Both pictures, big and small, need to be believable and they need to work together. For instance, you can't have an apocalyptic world where zombies have taken over, without addressing how humans are still getting their food supply. If zombies are everywhere, we probably wouldn't still have items like bread, because grain requires large open fields and these fields would be nearly impossible to guard and/or harvest.

EXERCISE 6: Give an example of the Big Picture Problems here. For an example: If there was a worldwide zombie apocalypse, nations around the world would lose communication with one another and, as a result, the chance of them being able to work together for a solution would be next to zero. But find a way to explain the Big Picture Problems in your world here:

____

____

____

____

____

Now, give an example of what the Small Picture Problems would be in your world. For example, in the above zombie apocalypse scenario, how would it feel for your main character if she lost contact with her husband, who was serving in the military in another country?

FINAL THOUGHTS:

I've just revealed my six, secret world-building tips. What about you? What writing rules do you try to live by when world-building? Whatever methods you decide to use, remember to avoid that stereotypical speculative fiction wormhole: The Information Dump.

CHAPTER TWO: HOW TO IMPROVE YOUR STORY PREMISE BY ASKING "WHAT IF?"

Writing a book is all about taking an idea and playing with it. Sort of like entertaining a cat with a string. You move the string and the cat follows. You start with an idea—what if dogs could fly?—and then you move through your story, seeing what would happen as a result.

Even though there are no new ideas (all of our ideas are based on something already in existence), you can still come up with something that *feels* new and fresh. Part of this is accomplished by world-building, part of it is accomplished by creating three-dimensional characters. But a lot of times, it all comes down to that original idea or premise, the 'what if' that spawned your book in the first place.

EXERCISE:

If you haven't done it already, write down the original premise for your story here.

____

____

____

____

____

____

____

____

____

____

———————————————————————————

———————————————————————————

———————————————————————————

———————————————————————————

———————————————————————————

ONE SMALL CHANGE CAN MAKE
A BIG DIFFERENCE.

The basic premise in my first novel, *Afterlife: The Resurrection Chronicles* was "What if people didn't have to die?" The world that evolved out of that single premise became intricate and complicated and dangerous. Still, in the beginning, the premise was a simple one-line idea.

If you've ever read any social science fiction—things like *The Children of Men* by P. D. James or *Do Androids Dream of Electric Sheep* by Philip K. Dick or *Fahrenheit 451* by Ray Bradbury—then you know that in these imagined worlds, *one small change can make a big difference.* It can turn everything inside out.

This was exactly what happened with *Afterlife*. Nearly everything in the world changed when I removed death from the equation. And yet, despite my one-line premise, halfway through the book, I knew that I still needed something else. I needed some element that would show what my characters had lost in their pursuit of immortal life. Remember the old adage, show don't tell? Well, my story was in need of some showing.

SOMETIMES YOU CAN IMPROVE YOUR
STORY PREMISE BY ASKING "WHAT IF" AGAIN
AND AGAIN. SOMETIMES YOUR BOOK NEEDS
ONE MORE CHANGE.

For me, I discovered that final necessary change my manuscript needed while driving to work. I passed a truck, all painted with pictures of children playing. The signs on the truck were written in Spanish, so I'll never know what the true purpose of the vehicle was, but I knew almost instantly that I had found my missing ingredient. *I had discovered the one small thing I needed to change that would improve my book.*

Before I got to work, I had toyed with the idea of that truck until it transformed into something dark and dangerous. It became The Underground Circus: a world-wide, black-market organization that temporarily provided people with that one thing they secretly longed for above anything else—children.

See, a world without death must also be a world without children. In the near-future world of *Afterlife*, very few children were allowed to be born each year. So inside each person was a hunger for the family that they couldn't have.

Every writer explores new territory when he or she writes. I didn't know until I really dug into this book that one of the tragic repercussions of jumping from one life to the next would be the breakdown of the family unit.

In the end, besides being a good story, *Afterlife* also became a cautionary tale: Be careful what you wish for.

· · ·

FINAL THOUGHTS:

Remember, you may need to ask "What If?" throughout your story. It's a great tool to use when struggling with writer's block or when you're wondering what should happen next in your story. It may possibly be the best tool available for a Discover Writer, aka someone who is often referred to as a Pantser, rather than a Plotter.

EXERCISE:

Write several more possible **"What If"** questions for your story here, ideas that will help keep your story interesting:

1. ____

____

2. ____

____

3. ____

____

4. ____

____

5. ____

____

6. ___________________________________

____

7. ___________________________________

____

8. ___________________________________

____

9. ___________________________________

____

10. ___________________________________

____

11. ___________________________________

____

12. ___________________________________

____

CHAPTER THREE: WHY ADDING AN ADRENALINE RUSH TO YOUR STORY CAN BOTH ENTICE AND SATISFY READERS.

The sun goes down, the clamor of the city grows quiet, and the rest of the family nestles, safe and sound in a world of incandescent light. Meanwhile, one person huddles alone in a darkened room, face turned toward a screen, eerie blue light carving shadows on her face while her fingers slowly tap out a message, letter by letter.

A writer is writing.

October winds blow outside her window, leaves gather

in shadowed corners of the yard and nearby trees sway, branches creaking.

The writer is writing a scary story.

Why do some writers always return to the dark side of literature, spinning out tales that make readers sit on the edge of their seat? Perhaps an even better question, and one that I'd like to discuss here, is why do some people love to read scary stories?

While, I can't answer this question definitively, I can offer some suggestions.

1. ADRENALINE RUSH:

This is my favorite answer, although many of the others are just as good. We read scary stories so we can experience artificial situations of "fight or flight." These scenarios, whether real or imagined, get your body ready for action by giving you an extra dose of adrenaline. Your heartbeat speeds up, your breathing increases and your blood pressure increases—in other words, it's like an instant dose of caffeine combined with heavy exercise. You're ready to leap over tall buildings in a single bound, although you may be screaming "Mommy!" all the way.

EXERCISE 1: Give an example of a "fight or flight" situation that could involve your main character.

____

____

____

2. FAMILIARITY:

You've been here before and you liked it. You've been reading scary stories for years, you have a list of favorite authors and you're waiting in line with sweaty palms when his/her next book releases. You stay up late (reading these stories is always better at midnight, right?), turning pages while everyone else is asleep. But the truth of the matter is you can't sleep, can you? Not until you know what happens next…

EXERCISE 2: Not knowing what will happen next keeps readers invested in your story. Give a few bullet point examples below of events in your story where you expect readers to keep reading.

____

____

____

____

____

____

____

EXERCISE 2A: Now that you know where your readers will expect tension, how will you deliver it? Can you ratchet up the tension, just a bit more, to make sure they don't put your book down? Things to consider: write short sentences, use less description, include strong emotions.

Give a few examples below of how you can make these scenes even more captivating.

____

____

____

____

____

____

____

____

____

____

3. A VISCERAL REACTION:

The desire to feel something strongly—no matter what the emotion is—can drive readers to these types of books. Detailed descriptions of eviscerated body parts in zombie stories may not get you excited, but there are plenty of readers out there who live for this stuff.

EXERCISE 3: First, make a list of what emotions you want your readers to feel while reading your book. Include the emotions they should experience at the beginning, the middle, and the ending of the book. Note: There should be a progression of change. Just like a character arc, your book should have an emotional arc.

____

____

____

____

____

____

____

____

EXERCISE 3A: Now, take a few of those emotions and show how they look and describe how they feel. One tool that might help you with this is *The Emotion Thesaurus* by Becca Puglisi and Angela Ackerman. Remember this exercise as you write your book. First, ask what emotion you want to convey. Then, figure out how to both show and describe that feeling.

4. TO FEEL ALIVE:

Similar to the previous answer, books that put you on the edge remind you that you are alive. You're not watching some soap opera at lunch time; you're hunched over a novel wondering if the heroine is really strong and smart enough to survive that demon horde that's been chasing her for the last twenty pages.

EXERCISE 4: What have you done or experienced that made you feel like you were on the edge? Have you ever engaged in an extreme sport or had an encounter where your life was at risk? How did you feel? Were you frightened or were you calm? Were you more or less aware of what you were doing? Did it feel like time slowed down? What about afterward, how did you feel then? All of these experiences can help you deliver that adrenaline punch your reader is craving. For reference purposes, put some examples of what you have personally experienced below.

____

____

____

____

____

____

5. TO CONQUER THE DEMONS:

We all have our demons, things we're afraid of but don't want to admit. Things like clowns (*It*), menacing dolls (*Chucky*), the end of the world (*The Stand*), rampant pestilence (*Contagion*), rabid dogs (*Cujo*), vampires (*Interview with a Vampire*) and serial killers (*Darkly Dreaming Dexter*). By vicariously facing your fears in a novel, you're able to tame them, or at least, imagine that you've tamed them. Until they show up the next night, waiting for you in the closet.

EXERCISE 5: What are you afraid of? It's okay to admit it here. Make a list and remember this when you're writing your next scary scene. If your fear seems irrational, like a fear of ice cream or laughter, remember to foreshadow it. Give your reader a taste of it beforehand. Show why it will terrify your main character later. Remember the snakes in *Indiana Jones And The Lost Ark*? We found out early in the movie that Indiana was terrified of snakes. When they appeared again later, we believed his terror.

____

____

____

____

____

____

6. TO EXPLORE THE UNKNOWN:

There are boundless supernatural realms, where wonder and horror walk side by side—realms where people rise from the dead or where someone learns the future in their dreams or where someone is given an extraordinary power. There's just enough enchantment and mystery to make you want to know more, and just enough danger to make you glad this is fiction.

EXERCISE 6: Are there supernatural elements in your story? Are there creatures that can't be explained or magic that's stronger than science? Are there mysteries you haven't told your readers, things they won't discover until the end of the book? If so, make a list of those things and refer to it from time to time when you're writing your story.

____

____

____

____

____

____

____

7. TO FEEL STRONG EMOTIONS:

Anger. Hatred. Fear. Love. Surprise. Terror. Repulsion. Empathy. Scary stories have all these emotions and more trapped between the pages, just waiting for an innocent reader to come along and release them. Before you know it, you're experiencing the same emotions as the characters. Although this is similar to Number Three, I felt that it needed be to addressed in more detail here.

EXERCISE 7: In Exercise 3, you've already listed the emotions in your story and how to show them. So, let's do something different here. Let's focus on classic phobias instead. They evoke emotions, too. Include only those phobias that will intensify your story—you don't want to go on a rabbit trail here.

For instance, a zombie apocalypse could result in power failures which could cause your main character to be trapped in an elevator. Claustrophobia would be a bad phobia to have in that instance. Once again, when writing your story, remember to foreshadow any phobias your characters might have.

____

____

____

____

____

____

8. TO PROVE WE CAN SURVIVE:

Isn't this why we read this genre of fiction? If you're reading about an apocalypse, it's possible you're subconsciously taking notes. So, if X, Y or Z ever happens, you're ready. Don't we all know what to do in a zombie/alien apocalypse by now? If so, why? Most likely because you've all been making a list and checking it twice while watching *The Walking Dead* or *Independence Day*.

EXERCISE 8: What survival skills can you teach your readers in your story? Give them an opportunity to get stronger, just like your characters. Maybe some homesteading skills could help them out. Or consider explaining what goes into a Bug Out Bag. Research is your friend in this category. But first, make a list of what your characters need to know to survive, then find a way to demonstrate their survival in a believable way. Research can be done after you've made your list below.

____

____

____

____

____

____

____

9.   SATISFACTION WHEN TERROR IS OVERCOME:

There's an unbelievably sweet moment when the heroine finally plunges a stake through the heart of the last vampire. Almost instantly, your muscles relax, you slump backward in your chair and then breathe a well-deserved, long sigh because, without realizing it, you've been holding your breath and sitting on the edge of your seat, ready to run.

EXERCISE 9: Remember to give your hero and your heroine time to reflect on what has happened. They survived. But there may still be work left to do. They may need to rebuild society or find lost loved ones. Write a short scene below, one that encapsulates the triumph and relief of victory, even if you—as the author—know that their victory will be short-lived. This is the kind of scene that can drive you to finish writing the book. And it can reward your reader for making it this far.

____

____

____

____

____

____

10. TO PROVE THAT DRAGONS NOT ONLY EXIST, BUT THAT THEY CAN BE DEFEATED:

What? Scary stories can give you hope? To quote someone more knowledgeable on this subject than me: "Fairy tales are more than true; not because they tell us that dragons exist, but because they tell us that dragons can be beaten."— G. K. Chesterton. Watching a character deal with the monster in the closet can give you the courage to face up to your own monsters. Yes, tales of terror can actually be uplifting, when written with that purpose in mind.

EXERCISE 10: This is where you can give your readers hope. This is where you remind them that they, too, are as strong as the characters in your story. This will work especially well if you've given your characters weaknesses that they had to overcome, combined with fleeting moments of bravery that lasted just long enough for that character to succeed.

What is the take-away from your story? What do you want your readers to remember? Write it here. But keep in mind, this will have to be demonstrated in your story. Also remember that the final words of your story should be spoken by or thought by your main character. This was his or her journey all along.

____

____

____

____

____

____

____

____

____

____

____

FINAL THOUGHTS:

Is there a story you're currently writing that might be improved by adding an adrenaline rush or two? If so, which of the ten categories listed in this chapter would be most appealing to your readers? Note: Consider writing a short story, using one of the mentioned categories, and see if this method works for you. Testing a new idea or method is always easier when used in short fiction first.

CHAPTER FOUR: HOW TO HIT
TROPES BY FIRST HITTING YOUR
GENRE.

"WHAT GENRE IS THIS BOOK?"

This is a question that authors ask themselves frequently while writing. Agents ask it when considering representation. Editors ask it when acquiring. Marketing departments ask it when trying to promote the book. Bookstore staff members ask it when trying to categorize the book and when speaking to customers. Readers ask it before buying the book and when telling their friends about the book.

Phew.

The problem is, when you're writing speculative fiction, all the boundaries seem to blur until you feel like you're cross-eyed. To give you a brief example, when I wrote my first novel, *Afterlife*, I saw it as science fiction. When my HarperCollins editor acquired it, however, she asked for a few changes—not many—and the book was then marketed as an urban fantasy. To me, that book will always be social science fiction. But to many readers, it's urban fantasy.

One of my young adult novels, *Fathom*, probably falls into the category of paranormal romance. But to me, it's fantasy. I never saw the paranormal romance elements when I was writing the book. They're probably there, but to me it was like a math equation:

Overarching coming of age theme + legendary creatures + mythological elements = FANTASY.

But then, I'm just the writer. Writers don't usually get to decide what category their novels fall into. They just write the best book they can and try not to worry about things like markets or categories or the dreaded Latest Hot Topic.

So, just for fun, I put together a little Cheat Sheet for helping to define what category the book you're currently writing might fall into.

CATEGORIES OVERVIEW:
FANTASY:
May take place in another world and often contains magic or supernatural elements. Does not contain scientific themes (otherwise, it would be science fiction.) Usually has

a battle of good versus evil. May or may not have romance.

Books: *The Lord of the Rings, Harry Potter, Game of Thrones.*

HORROR:

Can contains supernatural themes; meant to scare, startle, or terrify. Sometimes rooted in folklore. May have vampires, werewolves, etc. Also, may have a gothic tone. Sometimes written very beautifully, despite horrific subject matter.

Books: *The Shining, Dracula, The Haunting.*

PARANORMAL ROMANCE:

May blend elements of science fiction, fantasy, and horror. Takes place in our world, but often has other-worldly creatures, like vampires, ghosts, shape shifters, etc. A sub-category of fantasy and/or a sub-category of romance that contains experiences outside the normal or supernatural aspects.

Books: *Highlander, Twilight, The Vampire Diaries.*

URBAN FANTASY:

Usually has a contemporary urban setting—although the urban setting can be in another time period. Set in our world, which is often populated by otherworldly creatures or immortals. May or may not have romance. Is usually written in first person, and is often graphic, gritty and/or noir in tone. Considered a sub-genre of fantasy.

Books: *Small Favor, Moon Called, Dead Until Dark.*

•   •   •

SIMPLIFIED VERSION:

FANTASY: The creature lives in another world and is beautiful.

HORROR: The creature is scary and wants to kill you.

PARANORMAL ROMANCE: The creature is a little bit scary, but wants to kiss you.

URBAN FANTASY: The creature is horrid, and you need to hunt/kill/destroy it.

SUPER SIMPLIFIED VERSION:

FANTASY: Creature—yay!

HORROR: Creature—boo!

PARANORMAL ROMANCE: Creature—smooch!

URBAN FANTASY: Creature—thwack!

EXERCISE 1:

First, what genre are you writing? There are many more genres than those listed in this chapter, so don't feel like you have to choose Fantasy, Horror, Paranormal Romance, or Urban Fantasy. Maybe you're writing Science Fiction or Contemporary or Mystery or any number of others.

____

____

____

____

____

____

____

____

____

EXERCISE 2:

What books have you read in this genre? List them
below. It's important to read in your genre to understand
what your readers will expect. Also, this research will help
you later when trying to market your finished novel or
story.

____

____

____

____

____

____

____

____

____

____

____

____

FINAL THOUGHTS:

As I mentioned in Exercise 2, knowing what genre your book falls into is very important when it comes to meeting your readers' expectations. Each genre has a wide variety of possible tropes, and your readers are intuitively familiar with those tropes. My recommendation is to, first, write the best book that you can, while also being aware of what genre you're writing.

Then, during your editing cycle, pay close attention to tropes in that genre. See if you can hit at least one of those tropes while rewriting/editing. Sometimes, it will be as simple as adding a scene or two, or clarifying certain passages in your manuscript.

You can also study genres and tropes before you start writing, and then incorporate that information into your story.

Or a more organic method would be to read extensively in your chosen genre. That will help you to intuitively hit those tropes. If you're a Discover Writer or a Pantser (like I am), then the final method is what I would recommend.

CHAPTER FIVE: HOW GENRE-BLENDING CAN STRENGTHEN YOUR STORY AND PLOT.

YOUR PALMS ARE SWEATING, YOUR HEART'S RACING, you're tongue-tied and you're certain that whatever you do, this situation is only going to get worse.

The brief scene described above could be from two very different stories.

THE FIRST:

For the past two days, you've been tracked by a serial

killer. You finally make it into a Mini-Mart and you want to tell someone what's going on, you want to ask for help, but you're afraid they won't believe you.

THE SECOND:

You think you're falling in love.

THE TRUTH OF THE MATTER:

As strange as it may seem, many of the symptoms of falling in love are similar to those experienced during moments of stress. Queasy stomach, inability to sleep and lack of concentration. Is it any wonder then that romance often finds itself frequently mixed in with other, seemingly incongruent, genres?

WHY DOES THIS TECHNIQUE OF GENRE-BLENDING WORK SO WELL?

Most likely this method works because it gives the author two distinct plot lines. Whenever one subplot feels like it's cooling down, the other subplot begins to heat up. By switching from one plot to the other, the author is able to keep the reader on the edge of her seat, wondering if A) the heroine will be eaten by zombies or if B) the heroine will realize that the hot boy she's been hanging out with is really in love with her, and she feels the same way.

Another reason blending romance with another genre works so well is the fact that falling in love and fleeing for your life are both adrenaline-packed actions that are fraught with danger. Ever tell someone you're crushing on them only to have them answer, "I don't feel the same way." Life changing. You instantly wish you had a cloak of invisibility.

When it comes to storytelling, romance is a lot like chocolate. It goes with everything. It goes with mystery, horror, science fiction, fantasy, action adventure and literary fiction. It not only goes with these genres, it *enhances* them. It makes them stronger, gives them deeper themes, greater stakes, and higher rewards. *In other words, the addition of romance almost always makes stories better.*

Some popular YA examples of genre-blending:

• Mystery/Romance:
The Body Finder by Kimberly Derting

• Horror/Romance:
Ashes by Ilsa J. Bick

• Sci-Fi/Romance:
Enclave by Ann Aguirre

• Fantasy/Romance:
The Hunger Games by Suzanne Collins

• Action Adventure/Romance:
A Great and Terrible Beauty by Libba Bray

• Literary/Romance:
The Sky is Everywhere by Jandy Nelson

EXERCISE 1: In Chapter Four, you identified what genre you're writing in your current project. Now, consider what other genre might work with your chosen genre. You may decide to add Romance to Mystery, but you may also decide to add Action Adventure to Fantasy. First, consider what second genre might work with your main genre and write them both below.

EXERCISE 2: Now, take that combined pair of genres and write a new hook/logline for your story below.

FINAL THOUGHTS:

This chapter specifically deals with adding romance to another genre, but you can use this method by combining almost any two genres.

You can add mystery to science fiction, horror to fantasy, and so on. Have you ever written something that contained two plot lines or blended two different genres? If so, did it make the story stronger? Why or why not?

It's always good to analyze what worked or didn't work in one of your manuscripts. This is how a good writer can become a great writer.

EXTRA NOTE PAGES

I included a few extra pages so you can write more notes, if so desired. Feel free to use these for brainstorming story ideas, writing character sketches, or working on your world-building. Enjoy!

____

____

____

____

____

____

____

AUTHOR NOTES

If you just finished reading this workbook, thank you. This is my first attempt at creating something to give back to the writing community. You all have my heart. From the very beginning, I learned that other writers were the people who would be there for me, through thick and thin. Working with literary agents and publishing editors is amazing, but I must confess, no matter how much you love them, you probably won't work with the same agent or editor throughout your career.

Your fellow writers, however, are a different story entirely.

They're the backbone of the publishing industry. Without them, without *you*, there would be no stories.

I hope you find a tribe of like-minded, creative souls to hold hands with you as you venture forward.

And always remember, the world needs your stories.

PLEASE WRITE A REVIEW

Reviews are very important to authors and your opinion will help others decide to read my books. If you'd like to see more writing books from me, please leave a review.

Will you please write and post a review where you purchased this book?

Thank you for your help!

~*Merrie Destefano*

*Below is a sample chapter from one of my upcoming releases:
Strengthen Your Prose With Flash Fiction.*

CHAPTER ONE: Start In The Middle

WHAT IS FLASH FICTION?

For the purpose of this book, I'm going to define flash fiction as a short story or essay that's 1,000 to 1,500 words in length. Other books and experts might break this down into categories of different lengths and purposes. But we're trying to improve your writing skills and I personally believe the first/best place to start is in the short story/short essay arena.

BUT SERIOUSLY, WHAT IS FLASH FICTION?

Okay, to be more precise, imagine you walk inside a theater and a movie is already playing. Characters have been introduced, backstory given, and the action is underway. You're viewing a story in media res—in other words, you're seeing a story that begins in the middle and is probably in the midst of rising action.

This is what you want to achieve in flash fiction.

Begin in the midst of action, use a spare number of characters, keep everything simple, and end the story with a bit of ambiguity.

Flash fiction is almost like a poignant, important scene stolen from a larger volume. It tells an entire story, but it's been condensed, until it's similar to poetry. It packs a strong emotional punch.

HOW DO I START?

Writing prompts are great, if you don't know what you want to write about. It's also great to give yourself a time limit. Believe it or not, one reason to learn to write fast is it helps you to break through writer's block. One part of you wants to write. Another part of you wants to critique your work, edit it, change it, and maybe even stop it. Why? Because writing is scary. It causes you to tap into your subconscious, you dig up unpleasant memories and use them as fodder, you expose your vulnerabilities, your anger, your prejudice, your bias, your love, your pain.

In other words, writing—when done well—hurts.

So, naturally, some part of you might want you to stop.

Okay, that's my opinion. Other experts will give you different reasons for the editor inside you who constantly criticizes your own work. I'm giving you my own interpretation and I'm telling you not to be afraid.

Even if it hurts.

Write anyway.

You can always edit out the scary bits later.

You can change the names and dates and locations.

You can omit that part where you tell the world where the bodies are buried.

In my writing, I have exposed and fought against childhood bullies (in *Fathom*), given an abused dog immortal life (in *Afterlife*), helped a prodigal daughter avenge the death of her friend (in *Lost Girls*), and attempted to save the world from demon-like aliens (in *Valiant.*)

Choose your own villain. Expose them. Take them down.

In 1,500 words or less.

That's your first writing prompt, if you feel so bold to take it.

I took down a villain in my flash fiction titled *Dirty Jobs [Example One]*. It's actually based on a religious cult leader who encouraged his followers to abuse children. I really can't think of a greater villain than someone who hurts those helpless to defend themselves. But you have to choose your own villain.

Write about that bad guy/ girl/ organization.

Give yourself thirty minutes.

AUTHOR'S NOTE: I didn't include Example One: Dirty Jobs in this sample, but it will be in the final book, *Strengthen Your Prose With Flash Fiction.*

ABOUT THE AUTHOR

Merrie Destefano is a multiple-award-winning author who writes lyrical tales of magic, mystery, and hope. Her traditional books have been published by HarperCollins, Entangled Teen, and Walter Foster, while her indie imprint is Ruby Slippers Press.

She worked for Focus on the Family, The Word For Today, Engaged Media, and PJS Publications, and her magazine experience includes editor of *Victorian Homes* magazine, *Zombies* magazine, *Haunted: Mysteries And Legends* magazine, *American Farmhouse Style* magazine, *Vintage Gardens* magazine and founding editor of *Cottages & Bungalows* magazine. Her co-authored art books include *How To Draw Vampires, How To Draw Zombies,* and *How to Draw Grimm's Dark Fairy Tales.* Her edited books include *The Man God Uses* by Chuck

Smith, *Oil Pastel Step-By-Step* by Nathan Rohlander, and *The Art of Drawing Fantasy Characters* by Jacob Glaser.

Born in the Midwest, Merrie now lives in Southern California, where she runs on caffeine, and shares her home with rescue dogs and cats. And although she dearly loves science fiction, in her heart of hearts, she still doesn't believe airplanes should be able to fly.

For more information or to join the author's newsletter, please visit her website.
www.MerrieDestefano.com

BOOKS BY MERRIE DESTEFANO

Please visit Merrie's website for more information about her books.

Fiction:

Shade: The Complete Trilogy

Lost Girls

Valiant

Fathom and Fury

Queen of the Night

Fiction To Come:

King of the Ravens

Empire of Myth

Toil and Trouble

Wolf at the Door

Rebel: Valiant Book 2

Writing Books To Come:

The Goblin Journal

Heroes And Villains

Damsels In Distress

Strengthen Your Prose With Flash Fiction

"Highly recommended for horror and Universal monster fans, as well as anyone looking for a new twist on a historical novel."
—5 stars, Rose Paul

"The story is fantastic, the prose is dark and delicious, and Katherine Holt's execution as the narrator is exactly what I'd dreamed of as a reader."
—5 stars, Silvana

"Atmospheric, lush, and suspenseful—what more could I possibly want in an audio book?"
—5 stars, L. Mailloux

FAIRYTALE CHRISTMAS AUDIOBOOK

Outlander meets Sleeping Beauty in this historic tale of the Fair Folk and their exodus from Eire Land.

What five-star reviewers had to say:

"A magical story of the power of love and its ability to endure despite time and evil."

"Loved this rich tale of the fairy queen and the loss of her beloved Ireland."

"Fae, Christmas, and Folklore? What's not to love?"
